Who is the Enemy?

Also from Westphalia Press
westphaliapress.org

Who is the Enemy?

The Revolution in Terrorism Affairs and the Ways to Understand It

by Alain Bauer

Westphalia Press
An imprint of Policy Studies Organization

Westphalia Press
An imprint of Policy Studies Organization
1527 New Hampshire Ave., NW
Washington, D.C. 20036
info@ipsonet.org

ISBN-13: 978-1-63391-179-6
ISBN-10: 1633911799

Cover design by Taillefer Long at Illuminated Stories:
www.illuminatedstories.com

Daniel Gutierrez-Sandoval, Executive Director
PSO and Westphalia Press

Updated material and comments on this edition
can be found at the Westphalia Press website:
www.westphaliapress.org

Contents

Who is the Enemy?

The Revolution in Terrorism Affairs

D uring past centuries, wars and conflicts used to be easy to understand: a cause, an enemy, a war. Everything was clear, obvious and predictable. There was an evident symmetry between adversaries in terms of means and strategies. The enemy was capable of negotiating, of accepting compromises and of surrendering. Everything was simple.

This was true until the fall of the Berlin Wall. At that time, terrorism worked on a push-button system. Everything was connected to Moscow or Washington. When the 20th century superpowers wanted something to happen, to be interrupted or to disappear, their orders were carried out in all haste.

Then, at the beginning of the 1990s, there appeared a nexus that Westerners called "Al-Qaeda" (but which actually identified itself as the "Islamic Front for the Jihad against the Jews and the Crusaders", a much less snappy name, but more pertinent), which overturned previous terrorist methods of operation linked to the strategies of the superpowers. It was no longer necessary to obtain the support of a state in order to act. Al-Qaeda was a type of organisation that no longer had anything in common with other movements like Euskadi Ta Askatasuna (ETA), the Irish Republican Army (IRA), the German Red Army Faction (RAF), or the Fuerzas Armadas Revolucionarias de Colombia (FARC of Colombia).

The appearance of Al-Qaeda sparked off a true revolution in terrorism, whether it be in motivation, the players involved, in strategy or in organisation. It is not generally known, but the word "terrorism" is of French origin. It was first used in November 1794 as a name for the doctrine of the partisans of the Terror, that paroxysmal period of the French Revolution between the summers of 1793 and 1794. Terrorism then was a means of exercising power. Since then, its definition has evolved; its modus operandi as well. In the middle of the 1990s it entered a new phase, disconcerting the states that sought to combat it.

It is therefore particularly important to make an in-depth analysis of these Revolution in Terrorism Affairs, to coin the expression usually employed to designate developments in military strategies. We should concentrate on the very bases of terrorism rather than on any timeline in order to better understand what we have been exposed to for the last fifteen years or so.

From Kelkal 1995 to Kouachi/Coulibaly 2015: The emergence of hybrid terrorism

O n May 24th 2014, Mehdi Nemmouche, a Frenchman of Algerian origin, opened fire on the Jewish museum of Brussels in Belgium, killing four people. On May 30th, by an incredible stroke of luck, he was arrested by French customs in Marseilles in a bus coming back from the Netherlands. He had spent more than a year in Syria as a jailer for the Islamic State group and seems to have been sent back to Europe because of his violent treatment of certain hostages whose worth as merchandise was too great to be spoiled.

On January 7th 2015, the Kouachi brothers, Saïd and Chérif–French nationals–organised and carried out the attack on the *Charlie Hebdo* magazine, killing eleven people and wounding eleven others at the magazine's head office, then executing a police officer who had come to the rescue. Amedy Coulibaly, the presumed organiser of the attack, then killed a female police officer the following day and, on January 9th, killed four customers in a kosher supermarket. Amedy Coulibaly was furthermore suspected of having attempted to kill a jogger on the evening of January 7th and also to have organised a car bomb attack on January 8th. All of the attackers were killed by the police during sieges during which they sought to die.

The Kouachi brothers had lived in the northern part of Paris, in the Buttes-Chaumont quarter, and had met a group of young Muslims there who were being radicalised at the local mosque. It was also there that they met Farid Benyettou, a charismatic figure who pushed them into an increasingly rigorous way in religion and then radicalised them so that they would fight against the Americans in Iraq.

They were arrested in 2005 and Chérif Kouachi was sentenced to prison where he met a central figure of what is commonly called the Al-Qaeda network in Europe, Djamel Beghal, in prison for having attempted to attack the American Embassy in Paris in 2001. Already in this same prison was a criminal gang leader from the Grande Borne housing project in Grigny in the southern suburbs of Paris, Amedy Coulibaly, at that time known only for his criminal activities.

Beghal was freed in 2009 and began to receive visits from the Kouachi brothers and Coulibaly at his home outside the Paris area, where he lived under a compulsory order of residence. They gave him money and food and were joined by Coulibaly's girlfriend,

Hayat Boumedienne, who turned up again in 2015. In 2010, they tried to organise the escape of an important Algerian terrorist, Smaïn Aït Ali Belkacem. They were arrested and most of them convicted. But the Kouachi brothers were not convicted, for lack of sufficient proof for the judges. The Kouachi brothers claimed responsibility for the January 2015 attacks in the name of Anwar-Al-Awliki, an American Al-Qaeda evangelist in the Arab Peninsula (AQPA) who was killed at the end of 2011 (and whom at least one of the brothers probably met in Yemen during the summer of 2011) and Amedy Coulibaly draped himself in the flag of the Islamic State in a vivid video released after his death. It seems that this was the first combined operation mounted by members of organisations that detested each other and were waging a brutal leadership war against each other.

...but this was not the first time that operators of this type had emerged

On July 11, 1995, the Imam of a Paris mosque was assassinated. A few days later, on July 15th, shots were fired against the police in Bron, near Lyons. Then on July 25th, a bomb went off in the RER [the Paris suburban train/underground network]. On August 17th, an explosive device ravaged the Place de l'Étoile, where the Arc de Triomphe stands. On August 26th, there was a failed attack against a TGV [a high-speed train]. On September 7th, there was a bomb attack on a Jewish school in Villeurbane, near Lyons. On October 6th, a gas bottle exploded in the Paris metro. On October 17th, another explosion in the RER. Fingerprints on the TGV bomb identified the perpetrator as Khaled

Kelkal, an Algerian immigrant living in Lyons. He died whilst resisting arrest by gendarmes.

Kelkal was the first "hybrid" terrorist—half terrorist, half criminal—to appear in France. He was born in 1971 in Mostaganem, Algeria and arrived with his family in Vaulx-en-Velin, in the suburbs of Lyons, whilst he was still a child. As a teenager, he became a delinquent. His older brother, Nouredine, was sentenced to nine years in prison for armed robbery. In 1990, the young Khaled was put on four months parole for trading in stolen cars. A few months later, he was arrested for carjacking and sentenced to four years in prison. During his incarceration, he associated with Islamists who were recruiting for radical organisations in Algeria. After his release, Kelkal regularly attended the Bilal mosque in Vaulx-en-Velin, whose Imam was the fundamentalist Mohamed Minta. In 1993, Kelkal went to Algeria where he was recruited by one of the radical branches of the GIA (The Armed Islamic Group), headed by Djamel Zitouni, whose aim was to "punish France."

At almost the same time, Lionel Dumont, a former soldier, converted to Islam after serving in the peace-keeping forces in Somalia. He had joined the army in 1992, before turning to Islam. He took the name Abu Hamza and joined the Bosnian Mujahideen in the Yugoslavian civil war. Then he was accused of having been one of the members of the Roubaix gang who had made an unsuccessful attempt to set off a bomb at the G7 summit in Lille in March 1996. Another member of the gang was Christophe Caze, a French medical student, who had also converted to Islam and had also fought in Bosnia. This "cell", which included Bosnian Mujahideen, began its activities in 1996 in order to amass the necessary financial resources.

On January 29th, 1996, the gang members stole a car and shot at police with an assault rifle, wounding one of the officers. On February 8th, they robbed a supermarket and managed to escape from the police, mortally wounding a motorist, Hamoud Feddal, whose car they took. On March 25th, eight members of the gang attacked an armoured car but had to make their getaway before getting their hands on the money. On March 28th, the same gang members parked a car containing four bottles of propane gas attached to a detonator next to a police station in Lille. The bomb malfunctioned and only the car was destroyed in the explosion. The next day, RAID, the French anti-terrorist arm of the French police, attacked the gang's hideout. After an intense exchange of fire, the roof of the house collapsed. Four terrorists were killed and two police officers wounded. The other gang members managed to escape but Caze was killed a few hours later by the Belgian police. Dumont had quite a different destiny. Sentenced to 20 years in prison in the early 1990s for the murder of a Bosnian police officer, he managed to escape from prison in Sarajevo. He took refuge in Japan in 2002 where he led an untroubled life thanks to a fake passport which allowed him to leave and re-enter the country as he pleased. In 2003, he was arrested in Germany and extradited to France where he was finally sentenced to 25 years in prison.

For the second time, hybrid terrorists were at work in France, but undetected by the intelligence services and soon forgotten. This wave of attacks was the precursor of the events of 2001, linked to the assassination of Massoud and the terrorist operations that ensued. The only difference was that the 2001 operations were led by "pure terrorists," with no criminal past.

The response of the French government was totally different from that in 1986. The police and the intelligence services managed to dismantle the functioning, the organisation, the strategy and the modus operandi of the network thanks to the support of an informal international cooperation arrangement set up by the anti-terrorist judge Jean-Louis Bruguière.

The so-called "Al-Qaeda" cells in Europe

———◆———

The arrest of Djamel Beghal in July 2001 at Dubai airport as he was in transit between Pakistan and France on a fake passport, brought to light the existence of Al-Qaeda cells in Europe. These cells had already been described by Fateh Kamel, an Algerian-Canadian who had fought against the Soviets in Afghanistan, then in Bosnia where he met Caze. He had been arrested in Jordan in 1999 and was extradited to France where he negotiated his early release. Beghal admitted having taken part in a planned attack on the American embassy in Paris, although he retracted this statement shortly afterwards. In October 2001, he stated to Jean-Louis Bruguière that he had met Bin Laden in Afghanistan and had prepared a suicide attack. In March 2005, Beghal was sentenced to 10 years imprisonment for the planned attack on the embassy, with five accomplices. His mentor was Abu Hamza al-Masri, Imam of the Finsbury Park Mosque in London.

Most of the terrorist groups of the 1990s became totally autonomous, linked by a common ideology but without any claims to land or political sovereignty. They adhered to a mythology born of a radical interpretation of the Koran. As we have seen from the attacks on American embassies in Africa (Tanzania and Kenya in August 1998), on a US Navy destroyer off Aden in 2000, in Peru, Pakistan, Uzbekistan, Saudi Arabia and in Europe (e.g. in Strasbourg), these groups carry out or plan to carry out spectacular attacks throughout the whole world. The attacks of September 11th, 2001, which followed the assassination of Commander Massoud, showed the capacity of the terrorist networks operating with the Al-Qaeda nexus to carry out simultaneous attacks on American soil.

The overall conception of the operation was the work of Ramzi Yousef, who had previously organised the first attack on the World Trade Center in 1993. His spectacular Bojinka operation, which envisioned the hijacking and destruction of numerous airplanes, was planned with his uncle Khalid Sheikh Mohammed when they were in the Philippines, and utilized terrorist methods that had been developed in Lebanon in the 1980s.

The simultaneous nature of the attacks increased the level of risk but implied no real change in the modus operandi. For the first time since contemporary terrorism emerged, state terrorism or terrorism linked to a struggle for the conquest of power over a territory or a culture gave birth to an obscure entity, powered by radical, escatological and theological thought focussed on one sole objective – the kingdom of Heaven on Earth, a belief which could not be attenuated by any form of negotiated compromise. Although Bin Laden did not go as far as setting up a Caliphate, others went further.

From political terrorism to "gangsterrorism"

In 2002, my colleague Xavier Raufer published a piece entitled, "Organised Crime 1995-2002: Mafias, Cartels, Gangsterrorism." Notably, he wrote,

> The world of crime has changed…Two territories, up to now perfectly distinct–the "political" territory on the one hand, the "mafia" territory on the other— have amalgamated into one. The end of the bipolar world has brought down more than one wall… Other separations, notably psychological ones, have disappeared. The binary portrayal of yesterday's world–West and East, politics and crime–no longer has any meaning. Those involved in political acts (guerilla movements, militia, national liberation movements and terrorist groups) and those involved

in operations that fall in the realm of ordinary law (organised crime, mafia groups and cartels) which used to operate in their own respective territories, are now on the same world stage, obliged to mutate quickly or to disappear.

There are abundant examples of this mutation.

In March 1993, a wave of exceptionally serious terrorist attacks ravaged Mumbai, the economic capital of India. Thirteen devices—in cars, motorbikes and suitcases—activated by sophisticated electronic detonation systems, exploded simultaneously at the Stock Exchange, the head office of Air India, in hotels and office buildings, leaving 317 dead and 1,200 injured. Shortly afterwards, the police discovered in several hiding-places throughout the city more than four tons of C4 plastic explosive, several thousand detonators and hundreds of grenades and Kalashnikovs. On April 25th, 25 missiles and 32 highly-powerful home-made bombs were discovered in the suburbs of Mumbai. There is a bevy of armed groups in the region: the Sikhs fighting for a "free Khalistan," the Mujahideen of Kashmir and the Tamil Tigers. Which one was responsible for this deadly attack? And if it wasn't one of them, which terrorist group had such a stock of weapons and explosives? None. The perpetrators of this carnage were simply gangsters under the orders of Dawood Ibrahim, a "godfather" from the Mumbai underworld, who spent several years taking refuge in Dubai.

In March 2012, a few weeks before the French presidential elections, a parachutist was killed in Toulouse. On March 15th, in a second attack carried out on a shopping centre in Montauban, two uniformed soldiers were killed and a third seriously injured. On March 19th, three people, including one child, were killed in a Jewish school. The perpetrator of these attacks was identified as being Mohammed Merah, a 23-year-old Franco-Algerian, a petty criminal who had become an Islamist terrorist. Merah targeted soldiers because of France's involvement in Afghanistan. When his apartment was under siege, he also confessed to having attacked the Jewish school as revenge on behalf of Palestinian children, but this was a secondary target after he had failed to kill another soldier. The investigators were convinced that Merah's radicalisation began in prison and was reinforced after two visits to Afghanistan and Pakistan.

These spectacular episodes were a manifestation of "gangsterrorism," and it became necessary to analyse the phenomenon. Raymond Kelly, the New York Chief of Police, created the first modern terrorist intelligence unit in the West in 2002, within the NYPD.

In 2003, he agreed with my suggestion that the investigation of terrorist activities in Madrid, Amsterdam, London, Australia, Toronto, Lackawanna, Portland, Virginia and New York should be placed in the hands of a group of experts and police officers. Their results were published by Mitch Silber and Arvin Blatt under the title "Radicalisation in the West: the homegrown Threat."

This established that the radicalisation process comprised four distinct phases:

1. Pre-radicalisaion
2. Identification
3. Endoctrination
4. "Jihadisation"

Each of these phases is unique with its own specific

characteristics. Individuals who enter the process do not necessarily go through all of the stages. Even if the process is sequential, individuals don't always follow a linear itinerary. But those who follow it to the end are likely to engage in terrorist activities.

Dumont, Caze, Kelkal, Merah, Kouachi and Coulibaly – and, unfortunately, others who followed them – have been considered as exceptions.

The FARC in Columbia, the pirates of Somalia, the bandits of Karachi, some Indian gangs, the AQMI of Mali and Niger and the Mexican cartels are all now military forces who are not just imposing a "revolutionary tax" for political purposes. They are hybrid or mutant organizations. Most of the time, they are criminals; sometimes, they are terrorists.

Fakes, simplifications and mirages...

It is not always easy to come to grips with reality. Sometimes reality goes against established thinking and preconceived ideas. What is happening today is not so very surprising. It is a development in a chain of events that has been going on since the 1980s, but has remained unidentified. After each catastrophe or tragedy, a commission is created to attempt to understand the causes, yet the commission always concludes that the people in charge held almost all the necessary knowledge, but made a great effort to not believe the truth because it upsets the establishment. It overturns systems that are organised to react to what is seen in the rear-view mirror and only that.

For a long time, Xavier Raufer and I have put out warnings about the complexities of phenomena designated as terrorists, fakes, simplifications, mirages. In the Middle East, in Africa and in Asia, hybrids have appeared. Degenerated guerilla fighters, failed States, narco-states, gangsterrroists have come into being.

Westerners, marked by a form of imperial rationalism, have not sought to understand or simply get to know their adversary, but have preferred to invent one that suited them. This comfortable enemy is therefore fought against not in terms of what he is, but in terms of what the West wishes he were, and the media has decided to believe it. From what was called Al-Quaida to what one does not want to call the Islamic State or the Caliphate, there has been a huge reluctance to understand reality. However, by using history and culture to help put things in perspective, one can shine a light on current events, for what is going on in Iraq and in Syria has little to do with the West and its interests.

Dropping their ally the Shah of Iran in 1979 (as they would subsequently do in Iraq, Egypt and Tunisia), the United States allowed the return of a strong Shiite power which relegated the Persian Empire to a secondary role and consecrated the kingdom of Saudi Arabia as the new Guardian of the Gulf and its resources.

In 2010, by going along the path of negotiation with Iran, the United States disestablished their relationship with the Saudi Arabians who had no wish to give domination back to Iran, even less so after the events in Bahrain (the "little sister" of Saudi Arabia according to its leaders) where the population–for the most part Shiite, aided by their neighbour Iran–attempted to gain their share of power.

Hesitating between arming themselves with nuclear weapons (from their Sunni brothers in Pakistan who had already helped Northern Korea), getting closer to China which seemed a more trustworthy potential ally, and fighting directly in situ, the Sunni monarchies, for once united, decided to allow the establishment of a holy alliance that brought together traditional jihadists, former Baath party members and soldiers of Saddam Hussein, mercenaries from other combat zones, such as Algeria, Chechnya, and Bosnia which has taken control of an immense area. Yet their other options remain available.

Shiites, Alawites and diverse minorities came together to resist the Sunni offensive, under the stunned gaze of the Americans, who understood only too late that nation building is a risky business. The Ottoman Empire (Turkey) is wondering about its own role because of the problem posed by the emergence of an independent Kurdistan. The diplomatic freezer that was opened after the fall of the Berlin wall in 1989 is still melting, revealing everywhere the inanity of boundaries dating from the colonial era, of frontiers created with a ruler, and the remains of artificial separations imposed by defunct empires, particularly by our British friends.

The new Battle of Karbala

Today we are in the middle of a new Battle of Karbala. The first one took place on 10th October 680 in Iraq. It opposed Caliph Yazid and Husayn (Hussein), son of Ali and grandson of the prophet Mohammed who had refused to recognise the Caliph and take the oath of allegiance. The battle went in the Caliph's favour and Husayn was decapitated.

Henri Tincq gave a perfect evocation of the nature and impact of this battle in *Le Monde*:

> Karbala was more of a skirmish than a pitched battle. Nevertheless, it decided the course of history[...] Out of its first blooding at Karbala was born Shiite piety, fascinated by mourning and matrydom. Shiites made Karbala into a place of the supreme consensual sacrifice, and made Hussein into a brave

soldier defending his freedom and honour, ready to die for the sake of the original purity of Islam. [...]

Although Mohammed, the last of the prophets –the "Seal"–could have no successor, the leadership of the burgeoning empire was greatly coveted. He did not explicitly designate any one successor. After his funeral in 632 in Saqifa, near Medina, two opposing claimants claimed legitimacy: the companions of the Prophet, the Sahaba, men of experience, the first converts according to Sunni tradition, a sort of tribal and traditional legitimacy; and the minority claimant representing the Prophet's family in the person of the young Ali, a first convert too (but what is conversion worth at the age of nine?) according to the "Alides", forerunners of the Shiites (from Shia, Ali's party), a sort of Koranic legitimacy with a small following. The former were the winners. They provided history with the first three Islamic Caliphates (632-656): Abu Bakr, who repressed any return to apostasy, then Omat and Uthman who consolidated the state and conquered Iran, northern Africa and central Asia up to the frontiers of India. But it is impossible to understand the original schism in Islam without taking a close look at the removal of Ali which, even today for Shiites, constituted the first coup d'état, the first mistake, the beginning of the decadence of ruling Islam [...] Ali's caliphate (656-661) may have seen many achievements, but it was also a series of civil wars, the first in the history of Islam. The time of the *fitna*–the "great discord"–had begun.

There are some things that cannot be effaced from the memory of peoples and believers, and these may be brutally reawakened at the least movement that is a reminder of the pain of a past drama. When the

Saudi forces who intervened to re-establish order in Bahrain crossed the bridge between the two countries, they not only carried the flag of the Prophet but also had a very particular name: the Karbala Division. A sign, a message, a reminder. A promise too.

Whereas we can manage to forget the tribal era and religious conflicts, even if Ireland is not so far distant, they cannot.

The semantic question is an interesting one and the place occupied by things spiritual, secular, mystical, religious and the innermost search for ascendancy has a long-standing effect on political action. So it is that we become more interested in Babylon than in Baghdad when an intervention in Iraq is decided upon. We rediscover long-gone empires (those of Persia, the Ottoman Turks, Orthothox Russia...), we suffer the revenge of history and geography when we pretend not to understand contemporary conflicts.

In criminal or terrorist matters—but not exclusively —what seems to be news is very often what has been forgotten. This is also true for strategy. The adversary— the enemy—is no longer a single one. Time and space have retracted to fit the rhythm of the social networks.

Frontiers drawn with a ruler, the right angles of colonisation, have not caused identities, tribes and obediences to disappear. They have only masked them provisionally. And, in this ferment of worlds that we thought belonged to the history books— long before tablets—here we are brutally, sometimes savagely, having to face up to our mistakes or to the consequences of our actions.

Globalisation, commodification and sectarianism

We now have to try to understand why and how globalisation is profoundly and lastingly changing the interaction between politics and religion, bringing about dramatic upheavals in most parts of the world. The "commodification" of the world is taking hold. It is invading all spheres of life including the private worlds of the body and the sacred. Migration is undermining the social structure of whole communities. The progress of human rights and the free market are coming up against strong resistance linked to conservatism and virulent reactions linked to identity.

More and more people find themselves confronted by their own freedom and form groups of new "tribes" with multiple allegiances. They are submitted to contradictory orders in an ever-changing world. In search of individual or collective "solutions," they suffer because politics and religion are competing to mobilise them and sometimes to control them; at the very least in terms of symbols and moral references, but also in a more ambitious way, in terms of concepts–differenciated in order to be acceptable–of collective identity and superiority. Furthermore, Western states, weakened by changes in the world, often try to retain a part of their authority by disqualifying theological arguments in the field of everyday public life, whilst, at the same time, the churches have no hesitation in criticising the relative values that they consider inherent in modern open societies.

Thus we see globalisation initiating a new era of coexistence–not necessarily pacifist–between politics and religion, by tensing up these essential elements of "living together." Régis Debray, always fertile and precise in his expression, went further in the analysis of the cause of crisis and chaos with regard to the dilution of affiliations in an overall situation which is unable to meet the human need for identity and a sense of belonging:

> Our great thinkers did not foresee that the so-called 'global village' of the 21st century would witness so many villagers killing each other or so many neighbouring districts coming to blows. The spread of knowledge, libraries, the telegraph and steam engines were supposed to bring an end to the Tower of Babel. That was the basic credo of the thinkers of the Enlightenment; it was what Voltaire and Victor Hugo told us, as well as the prophets of world management and disenchantment (Karl Marx, Marx Weber, Jean Monnet, Jean-Jacques

Servan-Schreiber). The surprise is in the fact that technological and economic globalisation goes hand in hand with political and cultural balkanisation, bringing insurrection–for reasons of identity–in which the sacred has changed its colours. Letting off steam because of the arrears of history can even be understood as the consequences of the technical uniformisation of the planet. Hypercathexis about specific local issues compensates for the levelling out of implements, and the Visa card is mirrored by the identity card and the need for roots. It is as if people overcompensate for a lack of belonging.

The relentless drive towards the nation state

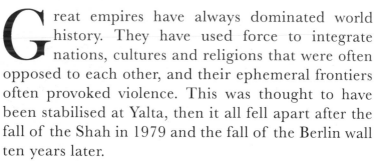

Great empires have always dominated world history. They have used force to integrate nations, cultures and religions that were often opposed to each other, and their ephemeral frontiers often provoked violence. This was thought to have been stabilised at Yalta, then it all fell apart after the fall of the Shah in 1979 and the fall of the Berlin wall ten years later.

The military decolonisation of the 1960s only rarely allowed economic independence. Whilst the Austro-Hungarian empire seems to have been definitively reduced to a post-Sisi nostalgia [a reference to the Empress Elizabeth], all the other empires are raising their heads again and challenging official borders: the Ottoman Empire, the Chinese Empire, the Russian Empire and the Persian Empire provide often brutal reminders of good and bad memories.

The Western creators of the post-World War II world are being confronted with the revenge of their colonies and the peoples they colonised. Wherever the British Empire withdrew–rather reluctantly– the mines they left behind have been exploding at an ever-increasing rate: Palestine, India, Pakistan, Afghanistand and Iraq.

In places where French colonisation attempted a less abrupt change, the situation remains unstable: Central Africa, Mali and Lebanon. Wherever the American nation builders made their mark, the price of their naivety and cut-and-paste use of ready-to-wear democracy is extremely high: Iraq, Afghanistan, Mexico, Central America and, more recently, Argentina.

On the principle established in 1945 by the US-Saudi pact signed between King Ibn Saoud and President Roosevelt on the cruiser Quincy, Westerners thought they could take advantage of the Arab Revolutions and settle old scores. But they bet on the wrong horses by getting rid of unpleasant yet flexible dictators in Libya and Egypt and by trying to work with politicians with close ties to the Moslem Brothers and who pretended to believe that they were an Arab version of Christian democracy...

Libya is in chaos, Iraq has lost its way, Afghanistan is in turmoil (if not worse), Pakistan, a nuclear power, remains a real enemy–a fact found out only too late by their American protector. Jihadists of all nationalities are on the up, boosted directly or indirectly by Sunni concerns in the face of the Shiite resurgency in Iran on diplomatic and strategic fronts. And transnational, hybrid organised crime is creeping in through the gaps left open by the protectors of a United Nations world.

As in the ex-Yugoslavia of Tito, carefully kept on ice by the combined efforts of the post-1945 protagonists, the global icing is melting at an ever-increasing rate. This warming is triggering the resurgence of ancient tribal demands for justice, land and power. Already, Persian Iran and Ottoman Turkey are finding their old status. Russia is reconquering its Orthodox space. Alawite Syria seems to have won its survival at great cost, Kurdistan is on its way to inevitable independence. No one yet knows what other things will upset the world map (Scotland, Catalonia…) since the thrust of peoples towards the building of nation-states seems bounden.

The Caliphate syndrome

Up to now, we have very often given credit to simplistic analyses which have portrayed our adversaries or enemies the way Westerners wanted them to be, rather than recognising what they truly were. We have created a comfortable enemy that suited our culture. We have underestimated him and ignored him. We have invented fables, like that of the lone wolf, to avoid understanding the dynamic complexity of hybrid operators—half criminal, half terrorist—in the field.

Since the Algerian civil war, the definition of the adversary, the enemy, is no longer obvious. Terrorism has changed, models have evolved and whereas the detection and gathering of intelligence remain at a very high level, analysis is extremelty faulty because it seems impossible for a Twitterised Westerner to take account of the complexities of the East.

We have given way to facility too often, and have very rarely put up any resistance to the sophisticated manipulations of the Algerian, Saudi, Turkish, Jordanian and Pakistani intelligence services which far outclass their Western counterparts in this field.

The forces of ISIL (The Islamic State in Iraq and the Levant)—or ISIS, Daesh or the Caliphate—have long been considered as insignifcant guerillas operating in Iraq before unsuccessfully attacking the Syrian regime, while creating problems for the "allies" of the Free Syrian Army. They nevertheless carried out several successful and spectacular operations in their conquest of territory in the north of Iraq, after having taken control of Fallujah for many months.

The whole Sunni triangle, and a little more, is in the hands of heavily armed groups that are increasingly well-trained. They have put to flight the Iraqi "army," which now only comprises Shiite units, whilst the Caliphate can count on the remains of the former army of Saddam Hussein and negotiates local control with Sunni tribes fed up with the corruption and hostility of the Baghdad regime.

One major player emerged from these events: Zarqawi, who seems to have managed to gain a posthumous victory over his main adversary, Bin Laden, and what remains of what we called Al-Qaeda. According to his biography, which should be viewed with reservations, Abu Musab al-Zarqawi was born Ahmad Fadeel al-Nazal al-Khalayleh in October 1966, in Zarqa in Jordan, which is where his warrior patronymic comes from. His family belonged to the Bani Hassan tribe, Bedouins dispersed throughout the whole of the Middle East, notably in Syria and Iraq.

The tribal aspect, notably with regard to the local borders–both complex and porous–must not be understimated. He was a petty criminal who became a street gang leader. It was during his studies at a Koranic school that it is thought that he discovered Jihad ideology and, like other young Moslems, soon decided to go off to fight in Afghanistan.

Al-Zarqawi met Azzam, founder of the General Services Bureau for the Mudjadeen, the forerunner of the nebulous Al-Qaeda, and then Bin Laden, but their ambitions seemed strongly at variance. He returned to Afghanistan, then under Taliban control, and founded the Tawhid wal Jihad (Unification and Holy War). In 2002, Al-Zarqawi settled in Syria after a period in Iraq following the fall of Saddam Hussein. On August 19, 2003, he claimed responsibility for the bomb attack on the building that housed United Nations personnel in the heart of Baghdad, causing the death of 22 people including the representative of the UN Secretary General, Sergio Vieira de Mello.

On August 29, 2003, the attack on the mosque of Ali in Nadjaf, a holy Shiite city, killed 95. In July 2004, his organisation suffered severe losses during the siege of Fallujah. On October 19, 2004, the Tawhid wal Jihad was recognised by Bin Laden as the "the Al-Qaeda outpost in Mesopotamia." Al-Zarqawi, now the local emir, was finally eliminated on June 7, 2003 during an American air raid.

Some months later, in October 2006, the Islamic State of Iraq was founded by the alliance of Al-Qaeda in Mesopotamia with other small Islamic groups and Sunni tribes in the Anbar province of Iraq. It was put under the military leadership of Abu Hamza al-Muhajir and the political leadership of Abdullah al-

Baghdadi (born Hamid Daoud Muhammad Al Zawi), presumed to be a former police chief under Saddam Hussein, "Emir of the ISI and Prince of the Faith," according to his official denomination.

The group distanced itself so much from Al-Qaeda that it soon became a fierce competitor and an enemy of Bin Laden's successor, Ayman al-Zawahiri, who never missed a chance to put a distance between them, to condemn their operations or to call for conciliation. After the elimination of Abu Abdullah al-Baghdadi in April 2010, Abu Bakr al-Baghdadi al-Husseini (Ibrahim Awad Ali al-Badri), an Iraqi in his forties, became head of the ISI (the term al-Baghdadi, "from Baghdad" is as common as Smith or Brown).

In April 2013, the ISI became the ISIL, settling in Syria after having absorbed a large part of the Al Nosra Front. Since then, it has gradually come into conflict with the Free Syrian Army and also with a legitimist branch of Al Nosra. This goes beyond the settling of old scores, which is more frequent than we think, between Islamist groups. The difference is in the very nature of ISIL compared to other Sunni players in the field.

Apart from being well-structured and internationalised, the ISIL seems to take as its model a sort of synthesis of Hezbollah, the Baath Party and the Bolshevik Party. It is a true pyramid organisation which exerts a rule of terror both internally and externally. It brings together seasoned brigades (Libyans, Chechens, Westerners...). Above all, it is characterised by its brutality, notably towards its closest enemies, activists who have remained loyal to the last group of leaders of what remains of Al-Qaeda, which had its swansong quite a few years ago now. In Syria, the ISIL attracts increasingly younger jihadists from the whole world over. According to recent estimates, more than 20,000. However, the war in Syria seems to have been lost. All the protagonists have known this since the victory by loyalist Syrian forces at Yabroud, near the Lebanese frontier, in March 2014. Even if it exhausted the combattants and their external support.

Yet the war in Iraq has just begun. Fallujah, Mosul (the second largest Iraqi city) and Tikrit (the heartland of Saddam Hussein's family) are firmly held by the ISIL, which proves resistant to almost everything and leaves only ruins behind it whenever it rarely retreats, as in Kobane. After the Afghan political disaster, the United States is preparing for its next colonial defeat. And, paradoxically, it finds itself allied with Iran in order to protect the Shiite regime in Iraq.

But we have to look beyond this episode—a mixture of national and anticolonial claims together with revenge of former supporters of the Baath regime and convinced Jihadists. For the numerous combattants who have come to the Jihad are like Zarqawi. They are petty criminals preparing to win back their criminal world rather than to proceed to terrorism.

Since the Algerian civil war, there have been very few cases of that happening. No one knows what really produced Al-Zarqawi. Manipulation, destabilisation, a Golem invented by the intelligence services and which went wrong as usual? One thing, however, is sure: Zarqawi's "children" are truly here. For a long time. And not only in the Levant.

Culture shock

The world that had been put on ice in 1945 began to dissapear in 1979 with the coming of Khomeini, the attack on Mecca and the first Afghan war. In 1989, Europe woke up to a new map. Since then, the deconstruction of states has been taking place, on the diplomatic as well as the economic front. Organised crime and radicals of all persuasions have widely extended their playing fields. With failed or failing states around us, risks of expansion, and enemies whose true nature is difficult to perceive, it seems time to return to a Realpolitik.

Terrorism has gone from the singular to the plural. We find the remaining terrorist professionals hesitating between retirement, senility and becoming mercenaries, state-created "golems" who have freed themselves from this to act in their own interests, hybrids born into crime and hoping for redemption through terror, but always in association with organisations and lumpenterroristes (often demented), and, motivated by a sudden impulse, deciding to take action. Here and there, rarely, we come across a "lone wolf" like Kaczynski or Breivik.

The world of terrorism is a compendium of players on the decline—more or less resilient—and of newcomers who force states' security services to rid themselves of pre-conceived ideas of terrorism in favour of new ideas: from ready-to-wear to made-to-measure. It is a real culture shock to come out of an obsessional Cold War in which we were basically looking for the spy who came in from the cold. That spy has not disappeared, but he is now relegated to the background by unexpected competition. And, from his point of view, unhoped-for competition.

Bauer

Alain Bauer

Professor of Criminology at the French National Conservatory of Arts and Crafts

Senior Research Fellow at the Center of Terrorism of the John Jay College of Criminal Justice in New York (USA), the Academy of Criminal Police of China (Shenyang), the University of Law and Political Science of China (Beijing)

President of the Higher Council for Training and Strategic Research (CSFRS) attached to the President of the Republic of France, since 2009

President of the National Council of Private Security Activities (CNAPS), since 2012

Editor of the International Journal on Criminology

Made in the USA
Middletown, DE
19 April 2015